THE HAPPY

WRITTEN AND ILLUSTRATED
BY ELIZABETH GRAY

Contents

A HOT DRINK IN
YOUR FAVORITE MUG

WRITING
+ STA

AT LEAST TWO
SOFT BLANKETS

HOME
START

A PILE OF BOOKS
YOU'VE BEEN MEANING
TO READ

A SUPRE
COZY SW

PPLIES
RY

HEADPHONES (PREFERABLY
NOISE CANCELING) AND SOME
CALM MUSIC

BODY
R KIT

PLENTY OF
CANDLES

SOME CREATIVE BUT ONLY
HALF-FINISHED PROJECT

ANIMAL FRIEND

I WAS A HOMEBODY BEFORE IT WAS COOL.

It's cool now, right? Sometimes I honestly don't know what's cool anymore. I'm more focused on what makes me feel comfortable—both in my inner world, and in my immediate surroundings.

Believe it or not, I actually started conceptualizing this book in early 2020, a few months before the pandemic quarantine and the year that will most likely live on in infamy as, "the year we all stayed at home" (as best we could). The joke back then was, "Oh, *now* everyone wants to know what introverts do for fun." But if you ask me, embracing one's inner homebody is about so much more than just staying indoors and avoiding people.

In a culture that celebrates noise, you will find me (softly) cheering for the quiet. In places where most see monotony and mundane, I find magic. And since home is just as much a feeling as it is a place, being a homebody is not a chore for me. It's a choice.

THE FACT THAT I OWN MORE CLOTHES TO LOUNGE IN THAN TO GO OUT IN SAYS A LOT ABOUT ME AS A PERSON.

Being a happy homebody is about being mindful of the moments that make up your life instead of rushing through them. It's about curating the elements that surround you, from the details in your home decor to your relationships and daily routine. It's about being alone with your thoughts, cherishing your quirks and creative spirit, and cultivating a space that authentically reflects who you truly are.

Being a happy homebody is also about being honest with yourself and others. It's about choosing what you consider joyful, instead of caving to peer pressure and indulging in the deceitful fear of missing out. In a society that favors the loud and the crowd, be the confident voice of self-understanding that says, "No thanks, I'd rather stay in tonight."

If you're a recovering people pleaser like me, consider this your permit to finally choose a different path. Don't go to the club, the high school reunion, or the New Year's Eve party if you genuinely feel drained by the whole scene: the noise, the obligatory small talk, and the pressure to "go with the flow" of letting others make decisions for you. Say "no" with confidence and reschedule once your social battery is recharged.

I created this book to salute and honor life at home, my sanctuary. I created it to shine a spotlight on all the joy, wonder, and self-discovery that can happen when you choose to stay in instead of going out.

Each section includes musings, illustrations, and activities to celebrate the indoors, both your inner thoughts and your actual interior space. Cozy up on the couch and flip through this book at your leisure, or keep it on your coffee table and pick it up whenever you need a dose of inspiration or something to make you smile. There's no right way to use these pages. They include a mix of reading, thinking, and doing, and you can enjoy them however you'd like.

Ultimately, I hope this book inspires you to take care of yourself and embrace who you really are. Because let's be honest: the best part of being at home is that you don't have to put on appearances or pretend to be someone you're not. You can dance as awkwardly as you want, wear your favorite sweatpants for days, or just...do...nothing. At all. This book is your permission slip to spend time with yourself and relish in all of the weird and wonderful things that make you *you*.

So, my darling: if you find yourself discarding your shoes (and some clothing) the moment you walk in the door, lighting what some might describe as "too many" candles, and sinking into your favorite chair with tea or wine in one hand and a good book in the other...then *The Happy Homebody* is for you.

To all fellow wallflowers and introverts of the world: this is our time. This is our moment to shine.

After all, staying home is the new going out.

Elizabeth

FROM THE MOMENT

YOU WAKE UP

EACH MORNING,

YOU HAVE A CHOICE...

YOU CAN GRAB YOUR PHONE, CHECK UP ON NEWS AND SOCIAL MEDIA, AND LET THE FRENZY OF THE WORLD SWEEP YOU AWAY.

OR

YOU CAN TAKE A DEEP BREATH, INDULGE IN EARLY-MORNING QUIET, AND MAP OUT YOUR DAY WITH INTENTION—USING YOUR PRECIOUS MOMENTS TO DO THINGS THAT LIGHT YOU UP INSIDE (INSTEAD OF THINGS THAT FEED YOUR ANXIETY). SIT BACK NOW AND DAYDREAM ABOUT WHAT AN IDEAL DAY LOOKS LIKE TO YOU.

What brings you the most joy? What do you need to feel grounded?

_____

_____

_____

_____

What makes you feel good?

_____

_____

_____

_____

my ideal day

- ❑ A HOT OR COLD CUP OF COFFEE IN AN AESTHETICALLY-PLEASING MUG

- ❑ CATCHING UP WITH FRIENDS & FAM

- ❑ A COMFY SWEATER THAT I CAN PULL OVER MY HANDS

- ❑ TIDYING UP MY CREATIVE MESS

- ❑ HIBACHI VEGGIES & A SUSHI ROLL (ORDERED IN, OF COURSE)

- ❑ MUSIC WITH A MOODY, FOLK, INDIE GUITAR FEEL

- ❑ TRYING WATERCOLOR FOR THE 3RD TIME

- ❑ GETTING LOST IN A GOOD BOOK,

  THEN REALIZING IT'S ALREADY MIDNIGHT...

your ideal day

Wake up with a sip of:

Quality time or conversation with:

Comfy clothing of choice:

Something productive:

Food that makes you smile:

Music that fits your mood:

Something to light your creative spark:

Downtime/quality time:

A GOOD
DAY

ALSO A
GOOD DAY

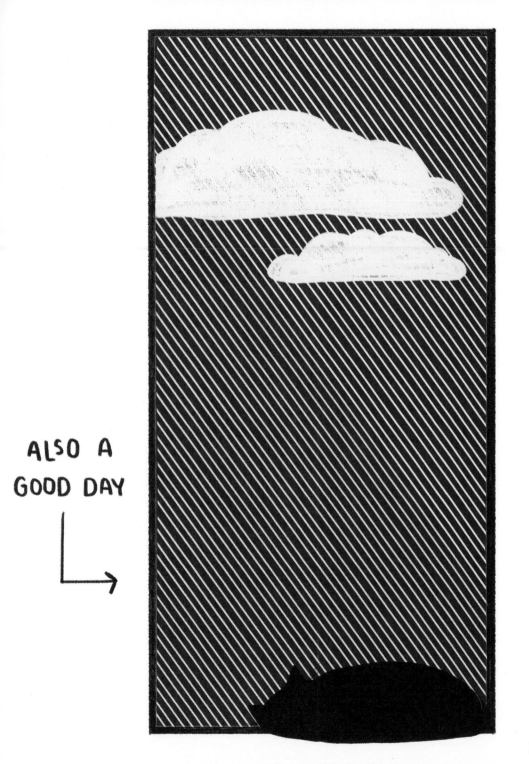

MAKING a house A home

Making a house a home is all about asking yourself how you want to feel in your space.

When you sit back and dream about your ideal home, what comes to mind? What feelings do you want your surroundings to invoke within you?

MAYBE your MOOD IS...

(circle one...or on second thought, circle as many as you want!)

DARK AND MOODY
CLASSIC AND CALMING
BRIGHT AND AIRY
MINIMALIST AND MODERN
WARM AND COZY
ECLECTIC AND VINTAGE

THINGS TO THINK ABOUT:

Color temperature. Are you drawn to pure whites and deep jeweled brights, or warm creams and homey earthy hues? Make a list of your favorite colors and tones and find ways to make them work together in your space. If you're feeling overwhelmed, start with a white or light shade, add in a neutral base color, then add in one or two accent colors.

Texture. Add layers with blankets and pillows in varying materials. Mix patterns that contrast in a clever way, like pairing a large floral with a small stripe. Style vignettes with items of different heights and patterns, like stacking pretty thrifted books with a bud vase and dried flowers you found on a walk a few weeks ago.

Odd numbers. When in doubt, take one out—as long as you're left with a group of 3, 5, or even 7. Chat with any designer or artsy person and they'll remind you that groups of items in odd numbers are more pleasing and natural to the eye.

LET THE WHOLE WORLD BE YOUR CANVAS

MODERN CROCHET

TAILOR-MAKE AND DECORATE YOUR SPACE BY....

FRESH FLOWERS OR FAKE + LEAVES

ACTUALLY PRINTING PHOTOS

HANGING IT UP

06 · 21

ADDING LAYERS OF BLANKETS + PILLOWS

23

A GOOD LIFE
WHEN YOU ST
AND ARE GRA
FOR THE
ORDINARY MC
THAT SO MAN
JUST STEAME
TO TRY TO FI
EXTRAORDIN/

HAPPENS

OP

TEFUL

MENTS

OF US

OLL OVER

ND THOSE

RY MOMENTS

— BRENÉ BROWN, PHD, LMSW

MATERIAL COMFORTS
THAT CONTRIBUTE TO
PHYSICAL EASE AND
WELL-BEING, SUCH AS
GOOD FOOD OR ACCOMMODATIONS

TAKE A MOMENT TO
DAYDREAM ABOUT YOUR
PERSONAL CREATURE
COMFORTS. WHAT ITEMS
MAKE YOU FEEL MOST
COMFORTABLE AND AT EASE
IN YOUR HOME?

Write or doodle your
favorites in the clouds.

MAKE YOUR OWN MAGIC

One thing I really enjoy is taking note of the sun's arc throughout the day and how it sneaks its way into different parts of my home. For instance, I like knowing that around dawn in the early springtime, I'll find my cat, Emmy, sprawled out on a large patch of sun-warmed kitchen tile, leaving her black and white hairs behind to dance with the dust in the hazy light.

I recently decided to add some extra joy to my days by affixing a suncatcher cling to the brightest window in my home. When the sun finds it, rainbow prisms dance along the walls and floors, and Emmy's coat seems a touch more magical as she blissfully naps in the warmth.

Some might scoff and call this simple thing childish, but when did it become foolish to find happiness in something as beautiful as a rainbow?

I want you to experience that same sort of joy, so I designed a suncatcher just for you. Flip to the back of the book, remove it from the pocket, and hang it wherever you get the most natural light. If you aren't sure where to hang it, try a south-facing window, which tends to get the most amount of light all day.

Then sit back, smile, and watch the magic happen. :)

P.S. DON'T FORGET TO CLEAN YOUR WINDOW FIRST—IT'S ESSENTIAL TO ENSURE THAT THE CLING STICKS!

MY MORNING ritual

SEVERAL YEARS AGO...

I was pouring my morning cup of coffee when I noticed that the hot steam was sort of dancing in the air. Its movement mesmerized me as I watched it curl around a sunbeam that was peeking through my kitchen window.

I had a passing notion (as one does) that I should film the moment, pair it with one of my favorite songs, and share it with my friends in real life and on social media. Thus began a new morning ritual for me-one that turned an otherwise mundane activity into an opportunity for gratitude at the start of each day.

My coffee ritual of pausing to appreciate my pour reminds me each morning that it's the little moments that matter most. We'll always be thirsty for more if we don't fill our cups up with gratitude and appreciate all that life pours out for us.

Speaking of finding joy in every moment, let's chat about mealtime… Sometimes I like to break up the routine of eating at my dinner table (okay, and at my coffee table) by planning a picnic right in the middle of my living room. After all, why shouldn't we reimagine the way we do things on occasion? And who says eating at home can't be fun? To me, an indoor picnic is just the kind of refresh button that a happy homebody needs!

A RECIPE FOR THE PERFECT INDOOR PICNIC

- 1-2 scoops of something healthy
- A pinch of indulgence (a square of chocolate, sparkling lemonade)
- Pretty plates and cutlery (why save the good china for one day a year?)
- A few of your favorite people
- A treat for curious pets
- Water: add to taste

OTHER NICE-TO-HAVES

- A blanket, tablecloth, or anything soft and cozy
- Pillows: optional, but +3 for comfort and style
- A drink in a nice glass—yes, even if it's water (Bonus points for using a fun-colored straw)
- Music for vibes, or an episode from one of your comfort TV shows

39

let's dish!

Before I made art my day job, I actually attended culinary school. I've always been interested in cooking and baking, and after designing a wedding cake at the ripe old age of 17, I realized that culinary arts seemed like a practical but creative career path for an artsy introvert like me. Through classes (and a lot of trial and error in the kitchen), I've learned that cooking a good meal doesn't have to be complicated. If you've got a few good tools and some basic cooking skills under your belt, then the entire process can be pretty easy (yes, even if you don't love cooking!).

The following are a few of my favorite tips...

SALT FROM YOUR HAND

AND BY THAT I MEAN, PLEASE DON'T SALT YOUR FOOD DIRECTLY FROM THE CONTAINER. BY POURING SALT INTO YOUR HAND AND USING YOUR OTHER HAND TO SPRINKLE, YOU HAVE MORE CONTROL OVER THE AMOUNT AND DISTRIBUTION. YOU'LL ALSO TRAIN YOUR EYE TO IDENTIFY HOW MUCH SALT YOU TEND TO LIKE ON DIFFERENT KINDS OF FOOD.

please don't put COLD FOOD into a COLD PAN

LETTING THE PAN HEAT UP FIRST CAN TURN ALMOST ANY PAN INTO A NON-STICK PAN.

PRACTICE Mise EN Place

MISE EN PLACE IS A FRENCH CULINARY PHRASE THAT MEANS "EVERYTHING IN ITS PLACE." BY PREPARING ALL OF YOUR INGREDIENTS BEFORE YOU START COOKING, YOU'LL SPEED UP THE PROCESS AND ENSURE YOU MAKE FEWER MISTAKES ALONG THE WAY.

A DULL KNIFE IS MORE DANGEROUS THAN A SHARP KNIFE

I KNOW IT SEEMS LIKE THE OPPOSITE WOULD BE TRUE, BUT A SHARP KNIFE IS MUCH SAFER—AND MAKES FOOD PREP SO MUCH EASIER. USING A DULL KNIFE REQUIRES MORE FORCE, WHICH INCREASES THE POSSIBILITY THAT THE KNIFE CAN SLIP.

OLD-TIMEY
BISCUITS

INGREDIENTS

- 2 ½ – 2 ¾ c. SELF-RISING FLOUR
- 1 ½ c. BUTTERMILK, ROOM TEMPERATURE
- 2-3 tbsp. SHORTENING

INSTRUCTIONS

1. PREHEAT YOUR OVEN TO 450°F.
2. ADD SHORTENING TO A 10" IRON SKILLET AND PLACE IN OVEN UNTIL MELTED (BUT NOT SMOKING).
3. IN THE MEANTIME, ADD SELF-RISING FLOUR TO A BOWL ALONG WITH THE BUTTERMILK. DO NOT STIR!
4. CAREFULLY REMOVE THE HOT SKILLET FROM THE OVEN, LET COOL FOR A MOMENT, AND POUR MOST BUT NOT ALL OF THE MELTED OIL INTO THE FLOUR + BUTTERMILK.
5. GENTLY STIR UNTIL JUST COMBINED...TOO MUCH STIRRING WILL GIVE YOU TOUGH BISCUITS!
6. TURN YOUR DOUGH OUT ONTO A FLOURED WORK SURFACE & COAT HANDS IN FLOUR.
7. PINCH OFF PIECES OF DOUGH ROUGHLY THE SIZE OF YOUR PALM, ROLL INTO A BISCUIT, PLACE IN GREASE IN SKILLET, THEN FLIP BISCUIT OVER.
8. CONTINUE UNTIL ALL DOUGH IS USED UP. THE SIZE MIGHT VARY A BIT.
9. BAKE IN 450°F OVEN FOR 15-20 MINUTES, OR UNTIL SIDES ARE MEDIUM BROWN.
10. TURN OUT BISCUITS ONTO A DINNER PLATE. SET PLATE ON TOP OF HOT SKILLET TO KEEP BISCUITS WARM.

According to my grandmother, this method
of making biscuits dates back to colonial times.
But all I know is that eating these biscuits,
fresh or leftover, hot or cold, takes me back
to when I couldn't quite see over the kitchen
countertop. My mother wouldn't let me get near
the hot cast-iron skillet at such a young age,
but she did let me set the table with whatever
sweet or savory biscuit toppings the family was
in the mood for. Snow days or summer haze, it
didn't matter. I could always find some of these
biscuits cooling on the
countertop or stashed in
the fridge for a
quick Southern snack.

FAVORITE TOPPINGS

- BUTTER + HONEY
- SAUSAGE GRAVY
- EGG + CHEESE + CHIVES
- AVOCADO + TOMATO

these foods can help you feel...

I'm not an advocate for crash dieting, juice cleanses, or unhealthy restrictive eating (and I'm not a dietitian either), but I *am* a believer in making simple, intentional choices each day to eat foods that make me feel better. Did you know?

MORE energetic

- Spinach can reduce fatigue.

- Apples can produce a calming effect, create more energy, and increase overall happiness.

- Citrus can help you feel balanced and energized.

less ANXIOUS

- Avocados are a good source of folate, which can help ease fears and anxiety.

- Salmon, eggs, and mushrooms can help fight depression.

- Quinoa can also have anti-depressant effects.

- Dark chocolate has antioxidants and magnesium and can help reduce stress.

- Almonds have magnesium, which calms the brain and may help alleviate anxiety.

A BIT happier

- Berries can stabilize your mood.

- Bananas can help you sleep better and generally feel more relaxed.

- Carrots can improve your vision and lower cholesterol.

GET YOUR CREATIVE JUICES Flowing

WHILE I NEED COFFEE EVERY MORNING TO FUNCTION, I ALSO RELY ON TEAS, SMOOTHIES, AND ALL-NATURAL JUICES TO GET ME THROUGH MY DAY. ENJOY THIS RECIPE FOR A TASTY MOCKTAIL ANYTIME YOU NEED A HEALTHY AND FIZZY PICK-ME-UP.

(Thanks to my friends Kerry Benson and Diana Licalzi, authors of the book *Mocktail Party*, for sharing this recipe!)

BLACKBERRY HIBISCUS Sparkler

2 TBSP Lime JUICE

2/3 CUP BLACKBERRIES

ONE CUP HIBISCUS Tea — STEEPED + COOLED

1/2 TEASPOON apple cider VINEGAR

ONE CUP SELTZER

1 TABLESPOON AND 1 TEASPOON honey

Muddler + SHAKER

ICE IS NICE

1. Muddle the blackberries in the bottom of a shaker.

2. Add all the remaining ingredients (except the seltzer) along with ice.

3. Shake vigorously for 30 seconds.

4. Divide the shaken mixture between the glasses (option to strain). Top with ice as desired.

5. Top with seltzer (1/2 cup per serving). Serves 2.

SIT A SPELL

ALL "CREATIVE JUICES" (YES, WATER ABSOLUTELY COUNTS!) NEED A COASTER TO GO ALONG WITH THEM. FLIP TO THE POCKET AT THE BACK OF THE BOOK AND ENJOY THE COASTER I'VE CREATED FOR YOU. :)

Put away the to-do list for a moment and go
hunting for moments of happiness. Making time
for play is just as important for adults as it
is for children, but it takes work. Just being
human is hard sometimes, you know? But it's
even harder when we forget how to let go of
life's heaviness for just a little bit.

Do the things that others say you shouldn't do,
(and who are they to tell you not to, anyway?).
Eat some cereal and watch cartoons. Be silly,
be impulsive, be creative. Buy a stuffed animal
or two. Paint your room whatever color you want.

To play is to follow your curiosities around
the corner or across the sidewalk, and to marvel
at the beauty and joy in even the simplest things.

So today, embrace whatever makes you happy and
weird and fully yourself.

RAINY DAY ACTIVITIES

+ PLAY WITH FRIENDS: BOARD GAMES, VIDEO GAMES (ONLINE OR IRL)

+ PLAY WITH FOOD: RECREATE YOUR FAVORITE CHILDHOOD TREAT, OR BAKE UP A NEW TRADITION

+ PLAY WITH PAINTS: EXPERIMENT WITH STYLES, TEXTURE, AND COLOR

+ PLAY WITH TIME: TRANSPORT YOURSELF TO ANOTHER ERA BY READING YOUR FAVORITE CHILDREN'S BOOK, OR WATCHING AN OLD TV SHOW OR FILM

SUNNY DAY ACTIVITIES

+ PLAY WITH DIRT: PLANT AN INDOOR HERB GARDEN

+ PLAY WITH LIGHT: TAKE PHOTOS WITH NATURAL LIGHT

+ PLAY WITH CHALK: MAKE CHALK ART ON YOUR DRIVEWAY

+ PLAY WITH POSSIBILITIES: LAZE IN THE SUN AND PLAN YOUR DREAM VACATION. WHERE WOULD YOU TRAVEL IF YOU COULD GO ANYWHERE IN THE WORLD? WHERE WOULD YOU VISIT? WHAT WOULD YOU SEE?

SEARCH THIS

```
Q  Z  N  V  D  O  W  N  T  I  M  E  Y  B  R
R  F  K  A  Z  W  Y  F  E  Q  I  Y  T  E  N
W  Q  R  Z  R  S  T  A  Y  C  A  T  I  O  N
S  L  E  T  N  O  O  N  K  B  S  Y  E  D  A
O  O  M  C  W  U  K  C  T  I  X  C  D  Z  D
L  N  A  L  D  I  M  T  L  A  G  S  U  A  V
O  Q  E  J  R  Q  V  E  U  P  T  V  T  P  Z
U  X  R  C  Z  F  N  Q  Z  E  K  I  I  M  T
N  F  D  M  O  T  P  A  K  O  C  B  L  H  X
G  M  Y  E  M  U  I  N  K  D  D  I  O  X  R
E  C  A  O  V  F  A  P  Y  N  N  N  S  J  A
W  Y  D  V  U  L  J  S  V  K  K  G  F  D  U
E  E  I  H  B  S  Q  S  G  N  I  L  E  E  F
A  M  R  O  W  K  O  O  B  C  A  D  Y  S  X
R  W  V  V  T  R  Y  I  N  G  L  T  B  Z  Z
```

BLANKETS	DOWNTIME	SOLITUDE
BOOKWORM	FEELINGS	STAYCATION
BYE	LOUNGEWEAR	TRYING
DAYDREAMER	SILENT MODE	VIBING

PROMPT PLAYGROUND

TAKE YOUR BRAIN ON A WALK AND VISIT YOURSELF IN THE PAST. SCRIBBLE, WRITE, OR DOODLE WHATEVER POPS INTO YOUR HEAD.

WHEN YOU WERE A KID, WHAT IMAGINARY LIVES DID YOU LEAD?

WHAT WOULD YOUR 10-YEAR-OLD SELF
THINK IF THEY COULD SEE YOU AND
YOUR LIFE RIGHT NOW?

ARE THERE THINGS YOU ENJOYED OR WANTED
TO PURSUE THAT YOU SHOULD REVISIT?

Paul Gauguin, a friend of Van Gogh's, supposedly once said, "Stay firmly in your path and dare; be wild two hours a day." The quote might be apocryphal, but the juxtaposition between the two instructions is just beautiful. Be wild, but only for two hours. Have a routine and a structure, but break out of it and be 110 percent everything you want to be for a set time each day. Stay firmly in your path AND dare.

As adults, we often get swept up by all the things we think we "have to do" or "should be doing" with our time. Routines and responsibilities are part of being a grown-up, but they don't have to dictate our days. Think about how you can build time into your schedule now—even it's just a few minutes in the morning or on the weekends—to switch your brain off autopilot and let your wildness run free. After all, it's the subtle shifts we make in our schedules that offer the freshest perspectives and inspiration!

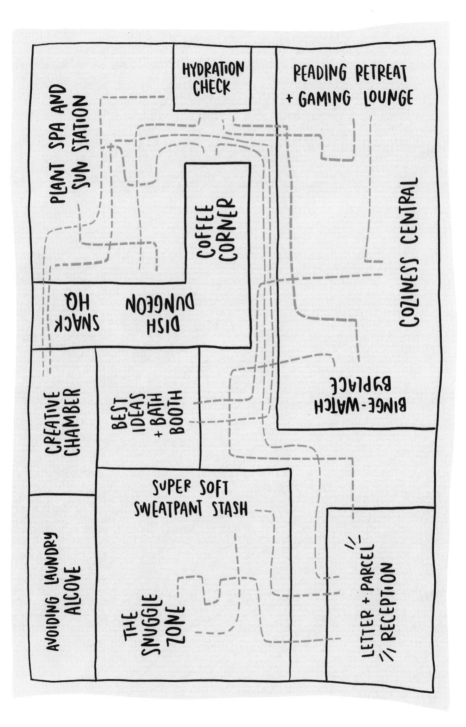

HYDRATION CHECK

READING RETREAT + GAMING LOUNGE

PLANT SPA AND SUN STATION

COFFEE CORNER

COZINESS CENTRAL

SNACK HQ

DISH DUNGEON

BINGE-WATCH BDPLACE

CREATIVE CHAMBER

BEST IDEAS + BATH BOOTH

SUPER SOFT SWEATPANT STASH

AVOIDING LAUNDRY ALCOVE

THE SNUGGLE ZONE

LETTER + PARCEL RECEPTION

view your home through FUN-COLORED GLASSES

AT SOME POINT, OUR CHILD-LIKE LENS SHIFTED INTO GROWN-UP FRAMES. WE BEGAN TO VIEW OUR HOME IN TERMS OF RENT OR MORTGAGE PAYMENTS, INSTEAD OF IN TERMS OF ITS PROXIMITY TO THE BEST CLIMBING TREES OR HIDE-AND-SEEK SPOTS.

BUT REMEMBER HOW MUCH FUN IT WAS AS A KID TO PRETEND ANY ROOM WAS A COMPLETELY DIFFERENT WORLD? WHAT IF YOU TOOK A MOMENT NOW TO REIMAGINE HOW YOU VIEW THE ROOMS OF YOUR HOME. WHAT IF YOU STARTED TO SEE YOUR HOUSE THROUGH FUN-COLORED GLASSES?

Without music, life would be a blank to me.

JANE AUSTEN

I curate a great many playlists because I love feeling
like a main character in some sort of movie, you know?
I tend to pick songs based on how the music makes
me feel instead of focusing on the lyrics, and then
I organize them based on what I'd like to listen to
while I stare dreamily out a rain-covered window. Feel
free to scan the Spotify playlist code at right and
listen along with me.

As kids, sometimes it was hard for us to ever sit still. Now as adults, we spend hours at our desks, hunched over a device for our work, often forgetting to even take a deep breath (eek!).

Gift yourself a few moments to stand up and move with intention and without inhibition.

Dance badly. Take a moment to try and do the splits (I never could, but I still want to try!). Learn how to handstand, or deadlift, or just do SOMETHING that tweaks muscles you didn't know you had. I really dislike exercising in the moment, but the way I feel the rest of the day (endorphins!) really makes up for it. Trust me, it's good for you, and your muscles and joints will thank you later.

Being creative can sometimes feel like a necessity.
There are times when we simply need to express
whatever is inside of us, just as much as we need to
breathe or eat or sleep or love (even if we aren't
sure what shape that expression will take).

But sometimes, we burden our fragile creativity.
We let the fear of failure or pleasing others get
in the way, causing our flame of creativity to dim
because we're too scared or too nervous to feed it.
And if you're an introvert like me, you know what
it's like to feel shy about speaking up or sharing
your creations with the world.

The key to letting your creativity thrive, though,
is to just sit down and create like nobody's
watching. What you create doesn't have to be great
(or even good). It doesn't have to go viral, and
don't you dare try to sell it—this is your time
to play. Stay creative without the pressure. Try
something new and leave the box behind. When you
open your mind, you'll be amazed at what is possible
with just your two hands and your imagination.

DO YOU HAVE THE COURAGE TO BRING FORTH THE *treasures* THAT ARE HIDDEN WITHIN YOU?

ELIZABETH GILBERT

- [ ] WAY AHEAD OF YOU
- [ ] HECK YEAH
- [ ] ....NO ?
- [ ] IDK
- [ ] MAYBE ONE DAY ☺

YOUR DREAMS

TAKE 20 MINUTES TO LEARN ABOUT SOMETHING YOU'VE ALWAYS DREAMT ABOUT OR HAVE BEEN CURIOUS TO LEARN HOW TO DO. WRITE DOWN A FEW OF THE THINGS YOU LEARN HERE.

CHOOSE YOUR ^PREFERRED LEARNING STYLE

AS EXPLAINED USING GUACAMOLE

(MOST PEOPLE FIND THEY PREFER A MIX OF SEVERAL AND NOT JUST ONE BUT DON'T WORRY ABOUT IT TOO MUCH, OK? THESE ARE JUST THEORETICAL AND FUN TO THINK ABOUT.)

VISUAL

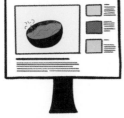

WATCHING A VIDEO ABOUT MAKING GUAC

KINESTHETIC

ACTIVELY MAKING GUAC

AUDITORY

LISTENING TO INSTRUCTIONS ON HOW TO MAKE GUAC

READING / WRITING

READING OR WRITING DOWN A RECIPE FOR GUAC

GARDENING IS ALL THE RAGE THESE DAYS, BUT NOT ALL OF US HAVE A GREEN THUMB. IF KEEPING PLANTS ALIVE DOESN'T SEEM IN THE CARDS FOR YOU, JUST KEEP THESE THINGS IN MIND...

REAL PLANTS:

+ Produce oxygen
+ Reward you when they get new leaves
+ But can be finicky and randomly die
+ Are prettier than fakes
+ But your cat or dog might want to eat them

FAKE PLANTS:

+ Won't get your hands dirty
+ Don't need water or sunlight, only dusting
+ Can be rather expensive if you want a good-looking one
+ But they thrive on neglect

NAILED IT

For me, doing my nails has become a form of active relaxation and something I really enjoy doing. Not only is it another artistic outlet, but there's also nothing quite as classy as the feeling of a fresh set. I'll usually turn it into an evening of chill fun with a mixed drink, comfy socks, and something comforting playing in the background, like my favorite episodes of "The Office" or the latest videos on my YouTube subscriptions. What started as badly-done coats of one color has turned into over a hundred bottles in not-quite-a-rainbow-of-shades-because-I'm-a-neutral-gal-at-heart and getting better at pairing multiple colors and painted patterns.

I still need to work on replicating those patterns with my non-dominant hand, but again: you don't have to be good at something to enjoy doing it. So if you want to make having super cute nails a little bit easier, flip to the pocket at the back of the book and enjoy the sheet of nail stickers I've designed for you. I recommend you bend the sheet and use needle-nose tweezers and to peel off the stickers. Once you've placed them on your nails, add some non-quick dry topcoat on top to help the edges disappear for that I-totally-drew-this-myself salon quality look.

Use Your Hands

Bake, but make it specific. Try French recipes, or only things with lemons in them, or something that takes days to complete.

Sand art. Yes, it's a thing. It's a messy thing, but it's a cool thing.

Paint. Whether it's watercolor blobs or hyper-realistic oils, just pick a style and go for it. Be messy and turn your kitchen into an art studio.

Sew old clothes into something new. Hack apart a few pieces and turn those threads into a new kind of fashionable.

Mixology. Turn making drinks (alcoholic or not) into an art form. (I'm sure you're the kind of person who has fresh fruit in the fridge or a bar cart in the living room...right?)

Play a new instrument. Find a used one you've never tried before and embrace the awful beginner stage. Practice with songs you actually enjoy.

Embroider (but not your grandma's style). Learn a few stitches and soon you'll be freestyling on jeans or jackets or a friend's backpack.

TO DO :
• CLEAN UP
   ...LOL 🙂

NEAT VS. MESSY

Research shows that working in a clean, organized setting can lead us to do "good" things, or, rather, what is expected of us. If your goal is to be productive, try tidying your environment and gathering your necessary tools, laying them out neatly where you can easily access them in order not to break from the flow state.

Messiness, however, encourages creativity and more out-of-the-box thinking. If your goal is to spark some creativity, try getting out all of your project supplies, make a bit of a mess, and see what happens. By releasing yourself from the confines of neatness and "how things ought to be done," you can let your inner creativity-tea pour out.

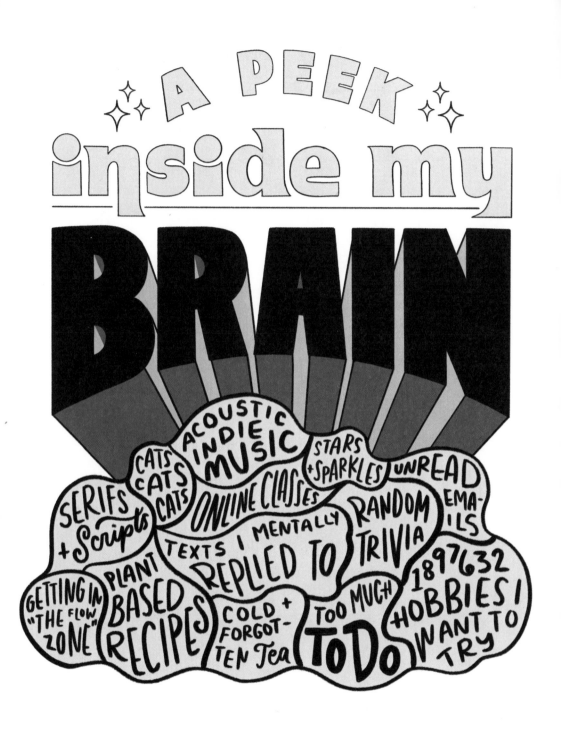

A PEEK inside my BRAIN

ACOUSTIC INDIE MUSIC
CATS CATS CATS
STARS + SPARKLES
UNREAD EMAILS
SERIFS + Scripts
ONLINE CLASSES
TEXTS I MENTALLY REPLIED TO
RANDOM TRIVIA
GETTING IN "THE FLOW" ZONE
PLANT BASED RECIPES
COLD + FORGOTTEN Tea
TOO MUCH TO DO
1897632 HOBBIES I WANT TO TRY

HOW TO GET OVER
BLANK PAGE PARALYSIS:

Let's face it: A blank canvas is intimidating as all get-out, especially when the internet is full of "perfect" journals and paintings getting completed in a "30 seconds or less" time lapse. The pressure of perfection is often paralyzing, so my best advice is to just toss that expectation out the window.

One of my favorite quotes from my friend, author, and artist Alli Koch is "If it was perfect, it wouldn't be handmade." So true! Getting your ideas out onto paper is more important than keeping the paper "pretty," so please, embrace your shaky hands and blobs of ink and messy lines.

One of my favorite exercises is to loosen up by grabbing a gel pen (or something with nice flowy ink) and just scribbling notes and thoughts and shapes and patterns and letters and words in no particular place. Don't take it too seriously. You don't have to be an award winner, just a go-getter. Have fun.

LET'S DOODLE!

Time for a little mindless doodling. Don't worry if you've never drawn a thing. Pick up your favorite pencil or pen and draw a few patterns in the boxes below.

HERE'S MINE!

KEEP GOING

✦ ✦

Now finish the squiggles above. If you can't think
of anything, stick to a theme: food, faces, animals, etc.
Show this to everyone or no one at all.
There's no pressure here.

A LITTLE
Lettering
LESSON

I'M A LETTERER BY TRADE, SO I FIGURED I WOULD SHARE A FEW TIPS IN CASE YOU EVER WANTED TO CREATIVELY EXPRESS YOURSELF WITH TYPOGRAPHY.

AESTHETIC

One of the easiest ways to start lettering is to try block lettering. You can do that by writing out any word (or just use the word I have here as a good starting place, and follow along by outlining each letter.) You can use the space provided on page 95 to practice.

Remember, it doesn't have to be incredibly neat.
In fact, the more personality, the better!

AESTHETIC

The fun part now: fill it in!
Congrats, you've just done some lettering.

You can stop here if you want and add cute doodles to
frame your work, or you can add a few extra steps.

Let's draw some drop shade, which, unlike a drop shadow, is closed at its corners to give the letterforms thickness. It is often used by sign painters to give letters extra dimension and personality. Do this by paying attention to where the light is coming from—almost drawing identical letters, just shifted slightly down and left. Connect them with these little bars.

If you want to take it EVEN a step further (I'm proud of you, whether you will or not!), you can add a darker shade or another layer of color or pattern onto the parts of the shadow that fall "underneath" our light source, the way a shadow would normally look with darker bits and lighter bits.

AESTHETIC

And now you can add whatever finishing touches you want. I added a dotted inline here, but you can also add doodles, illustrations, whatever you think the piece needs and whatever complements the mood you've gone for in your letter style and word choice. Remember, words + letter style = a story.

Practice your lettering here:

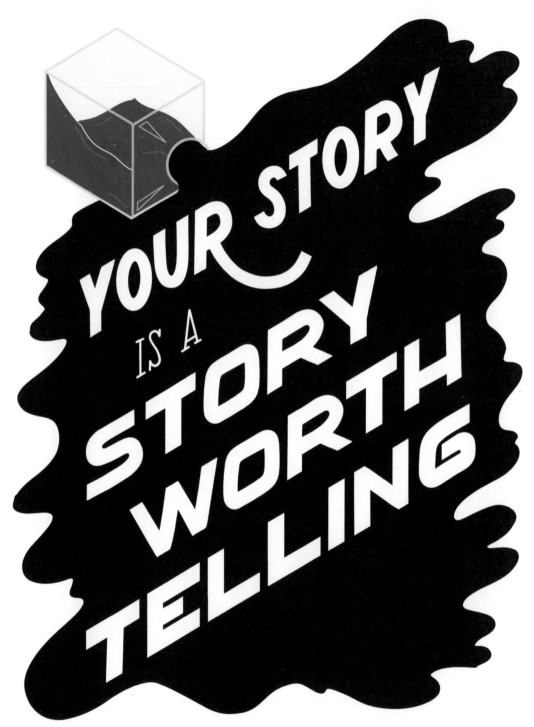

YOUR STORY IS A STORY WORTH TELLING

…even if you don't think it is. Your boring everyday routine is a refreshing change for someone else. That's why someone livestreaming their life as a bike messenger in NYC can be just as interesting as an artist demonstrating their painting process in a museum. You have to believe that your story is worth something. It's all been done before, sure, but not by you. You do have something to offer. No one else has your perspective, your history, your anecdotes, or your style. You and your life are a mosaic, a terrazzo of everything you've ever read and seen and watched and all the places you've been, not to mention your culture and your family and your wants and needs and dreams.

If your life were a book, what would it be about? Would it be a non-fiction memoir, full of silly things you said as a kid, a photography collection of projects you've never finished, or a fantasy epic chronicling all your daydreams?

BOOKS FOR YOUR MOOD

IN YOUR FEELS.

PRIDE & PREJUDICE

· UNCREATIVE ·

BIG MAGIC

WHERE'D YOU GO, BERNADETTE?

· SUNSHINE · HAPPINESS ·

· DEFEATED ·

THE FOUR AGREEMENTS

THE LIFE-CHANGING MAGIC OF TIDYING UP

· ADVENTUROUS ·

THE HOBBIT

· PRODUCTIVE ·

· CHILDHOOD NOSTALGIA ·

· QUIET RAINY DAYS ·

Wuthering HEIGHTS

PETER PAN

MAKE A LIST OF YOUR FAVORITE BOOKS. PICK THEM UP AGAIN FROM TIME TO TIME AND READ A FEW PAGES FOR FUN.

NONFICTION

FICTION

YOUNG ADULT

JUST FOR FUN

ROMANCE/THRILLER/ADVENTURES

WHAT'S A GOOD BOOK WITHOUT A GOOD BOOKMARK? FLIP TO THE BACK OF THE BOOK AND CUT OUT THE ONES I'VE DESIGNED FOR YOU.

WE CAN BE AFRAID TO BE ALONE WITH OURSELVES SOMETIMES. WHY? WHAT DO WE THINK WE'LL FIND, THAT WE DON'T LIKE WHO WE REALLY ARE? AS GREAT AS QUIET TIME CAN BE, IT CAN SOMETIMES MAKE US FEEL A LITTLE BIT UNEASY. BUT YOU CAN LEARN TO SIT AND LISTEN. SPEND TIME WITH YOURSELF WITHOUT MUSIC OR MOVIES OR ANY SORT OF DISTRACTIONS. YOU MAY JUST BE SURPRISED WHAT YOU DISCOVER BY STUDYING YOURSELF.

JOURNALING, OR WORKING WITH
ACTUAL PAPER AND PEN, CAN BE A WAY
TO ORGANIZE YOUR BRAIN. IT'S ALSO
THERAPEUTIC. JOT DOWN ALL THE THOUGHTS
THAT COME TO YOU WHEN YOUR MIND GETS QUIET
(DON'T WORRY IF THEY MAKE SENSE OR NOT)...

FILL YOUR
LUNGS WITH
BREATH
OF YOUR

WILLIAM WO

THE THINGS We Love TELL US WHAT We Are

ST. THOMAS AQUINAS

116

THE OLDER I GET, THE EARLIER "LATE" GETS, AND THE MORE I ENJOY BEING CHILL AND "BORING" (IF YOU WANT TO CALL IT THAT).

YOU GET TO CHOOSE WHAT YOU SPEND YOUR ENERGY ON. SOME DAYS YOU'LL GET MORE, SOME DAYS YOU'LL NEED TO GIVE MORE, AND SOME DAYS YOU MIGHT NEED A FULL DAY ALONE TO RECHARGE. SO ASK YOURSELF WHAT YOU LOVE AND NEED AT ANY GIVEN MOMENT—NOT WHAT OTHERS OR SOCIAL MEDIA OR THE WORLD TELLS YOU THAT YOU SHOULD LOVE. BUILD YOUR LIFE AROUND WHAT CALLS TO YOUR SOUL.

STAYING TRUE TO YOURSELF AND YOUR WANTS AND NEEDS ISN'T JUST SELF-CARE; IT'S YOUR BIGGEST STRENGTH.

LOUNGING ESSENTIALS

IDENTIFICATION GUIDE

THE UNIFORM

Does NOT include any
zippers, underwires,
or material that
could potentially
impact the supreme
comfort of the
wearer

THE SUPPORT

Comfort aid that can be added as needed. Heavier, fluffier, blankets that contain NO scratchy or purely decorative elements

THE SPOT

So cozy it feels like you're sitting on a cloud

☐ PILLOWS

☐ PET SNUGGLES

☐ SUSTENANCE

☐ PHONE-CHARGING CABLE

☐ ENTERTAINMENT

☐ NAP

TOO TIRED
TO BE
INSPIRED

DON'T FEEL BAD FOR WANTING TO REST. BECAUSE MAYBE, JUST MAYBE, NOT WORKING IS JUST AS IMPORTANT AS YOUR WORK. TOO OFTEN, WE TEND TO GLORIFY THE HUSTLE AND THE BUSYNESS, COMPARING OUR STRUGGLES TO SEE WHO'S LOSING THE MOST SLEEP OVER PURSUIT OF WHATEVER GOALS WE HAVE AND INTERPRETING OUR NEAR-MARTYRDOM AS A SIGN OF WORTH, SUCCESS, OR HAPPINESS.

BUT YOU, MY DEAR, HAVE TO CARE FOR YOURSELF SO THAT YOU CAN IN TURN BETTER SERVE OTHERS. IT ISN'T SELFISH TO TAKE A NAP, OR TO SPEND THE DAY QUIETLY READING AND AWAY FROM YOUR PHONE IF YOU NEED IT. BECAUSE THE QUALITY OF YOUR WORK IS MORE IMPORTANT THAN THE QUANTITY, AND YOUR WORTH IS NOT TIED TO YOUR PRODUC- TIVITY. MAKE IT YOUR MISSION TO CULTIVATE A LIFE YOU DON'T NEED AN ESCAPE FROM.

CLINOPHILE

A *Lover* OF RECLINING

THE Time You ENJOYED WASTING IS NOT Wasted Time

BERTRAND RUSSELL

CHILLING OUT IS NOT THE SAME THING AS BEING A COUCH POTATO, AND RELAXATION DOESN'T ALWAYS MEAN JUST DOING NOTHING. ALL OF US LOVELY INDIVIDUALS FIND PEACE IN DIFFERENT WAYS, AND IT CAN CHANGE FROM DAY TO DAY DEPENDING ON OUR NEEDS. YOU COULD BE AN EXPERT NETFLIX BINGER, OR CHOOSE TO RELAX WITH AN ACTIVITY THAT BRINGS YOU A SENSE OF WELL-BEING AND CALM, LIKE YOGA, GAMING, OR HOBBIES WHERE YOU WORK WITH YOUR HANDS. HOWEVER YOU CHOOSE TO KEEP YOURSELF CENTERED, REMEMBER THE ONLY GOAL IS TO GIVE YOUR BRAIN A BREAK.

A HOMEBODY'S
PARTY SURVIVAL GUIDE

If you have to/want to throw a party or small gathering, remember that you don't need the gift of gab to make it good. Quiet folks have other superpowers up our sleeves… like superb attention to detail, deep + existential conversation topics, and expert planning + list making, so let's use those to our advantage.

Set the stage. It's your house, your party rules. Do you want to have a deck-side double date with your couple besties with drinks + homemade charcuterie, or a sweatpants + Netflix snackfest? Setting up expectations isn't only good for your invitees; it can help you avoid stressing the small stuff.

Don't be afraid to set boundaries. a.k.a. "you're invited over from 6-10." Protect your energy with a firm end time if that's what you need (or if your guests aren't likely to take a gentle hint).

Dress to decompress. Wear an outfit that gives you a boost of confidence, whether it's some bougie loungewear, a bold red lip, or your favorite secondhand sweater. It can act like a suit of attitude armor and improve your overall mood, even if you don't realize it.

Plan to plan. Write out a list of everything you need to do to prepare, and if you can, schedule separate days for cleaning, grocery shopping, cooking, and more. Focus on turning each activity into something fun instead of a chore that must be done.

Play to your strengths. Don't care for decorating? Whip up a fantastic from-scratch spread that they'll be talking about for days. Stressed about current events in the news + media? Turn on nostalgic movies from your childhood and party it up in your pajamas. Whatever your host or hostessing comfort zone is, lean into it.

Listen to your heart. Just in case conversation stalls (or if you and your friends just tend to be okay with silence like me), have some background music to further set the overall vibe of your get-together.

Treat yourself. Make sure to schedule some time to nurse your social hangover + because you deserve it after aaaaaaall that effort. Do whatever makes you happy, like ordering in your favorite meal and NOT doing any dishes, organizing your closet, or having a homestyle spa night where you try out that new face mask you've been saving.

WE RISE BY Lifting OTHERS

ROBERT INGERSALL

Yes, you're at home, and you prefer to be at home and stay home. But spending time with the people you love is essential to show you care.

Learning someone's love language is a great way to know how to fill a person's cup (and your own). You can text your friends to tell them how great they are (words of affirmation), send snail mail or bake them a treat (gifts), give them a good hug the next time you see them (physical touch), invite them over to work on something crafty (quality time), or offer to help them clean their own place (acts of service). Even doing things for strangers, random acts of kindness, can fill both your cups at the same time. Doing your best to put good and love into the world can absolutely be done, even if you're a shy homebody like me. You're just doing it in your own way. And that's a beautiful thing.

THINGS THAT *might* FEEL GOOD
IN THE MOMENT BUT
AREN'T ALWAYS GOOD FOR YOU

- PROCRASTINATION
- BOTTLING YOUR FEELINGS
- FALLING INTO A SCROLL-HOLE
- BINGE-WATCHING
- REACTING QUICKLY + EMOTIONALLY
- "JUNK" FOOD / PROCESSED FOOD
- STAYING UP WAY TOO LATE
- AVOIDING CONFLICT
- SLOUCHING
- IGNORING RESPONSIBILITIES

THINGS THAT MIGHT *not* FEEL GOOD
IN THE MOMENT BUT
ARE USUALLY *Good for you*

- BEING HONEST + VULNERABLE
- PUTTING LAUNDRY AWAY NEATLY
- EXERCISING IN SOME WAY
- TIDYING A MESSY SPACE
  (NO MATTER HOW SMALL)
- A CHANGE IN YOUR LIFE
- EATING MORE WHOLE FOODS
  + GREEN THINGS
- NOT CHECKING YOUR PHONE
  FIRST THING IN THE MORNING
- GETTING UP AT A REASONABLE HOUR

INHALE THROUGH YOUR NOSE

BREATHE IN

& COUNT TO 4. HOLD.

NOW SLOWLY EXHALE.

1, 2, 3, 4.

IF YOU'RE REA

NG THIS, DRINK SOME WATER

GLASS CLEANER

Some mornings, I like to wake up and write affirmations on my bathroom mirror that lift me up and remind me of the good in my life. I try to write something that truthfully resonates and will make me smile despite how I'm currently feeling.

SCRATCH PAPER

If I'm feeling down about my appearance, then "Happiness looks good on you" feels powerful because, deep down, I know there are so many things in my life that bring me joy that aren't reliant on my outward appearance. Try this mirror exercise for yourself and see how you feel.

CHALK MARKERS OR PAINT PENS

Grab a paint marker or chalk pen and turn your bathroom mirror into a feel-good zone that reflects positive thoughts back at you (if you're a perfectionist like me, use painter's tape to help keep your writing lines tidy).

PAINTER'S TAPE

bathroom cupboard

It's easy to let ourselves think that shopping is the path to self-care. After all, there are so many products put in front of us when we scroll through social media, all promising to make us look and feel better.

Pampering yourself is important, and if you're someone who has skin, you should care for it. However, that doesn't mean you need the most expensive items or every last thing. But let's be honest: your bathroom looks like this too, right?

AROMA THERAPY

M

HANG OUT IN SOME NATURAL LIGHT

TAKE SOME SUPPLEMENTS

TH

MOVE YOUR BODY

SNUGGLE WITH ANIMAL FRIENDS

T A
SAGE

TRY OUT A WEIGHTED BLANKET

TRY SOMETHING NEW

WRITE DOWN THINGS YOU'RE GRATEFUL FOR

REIMAGINE YOUR FAVORITE MEMORIES

APY

COMPLETE A TASK, NO MATTER HOW SMALL

FREE SERATONIN

ASTRO

LOVER OF T

TAKE SOME TIME TONIGHT TO TAKE
NOTE OF THE STARS YOU CAN SEE FROM
YOUR HOUSE. ARE THERE A GREAT MANY
BRIGHT DOTS, SHINING STEADILY IN THE
QUIET, OR ONLY A TWINKLING ONE
OR TWO IN THE BUSTLING HAZE OF
A NEARBY MUNICIPALITY?

PHILE
HE STARS

RECONNECT WITH YOUR SENSE OF AWE. REMEMBER HOW TRULY VAST THE UNIVERSE IS OUTSIDE YOUR WINDOWS, AND BE GRATEFUL FOR YOUR TINY PLACE AMIDST THE MAGIC OF IT ALL. KEEP YOUR FEET ON THE GROUND, BUT LET YOUR HEART AND THOUGHTS AND DREAMS FLY AMONG THE STARS, MY DEAR.

I HAVE
THAT
LOVE
LIFE WI
YOU I

arthur

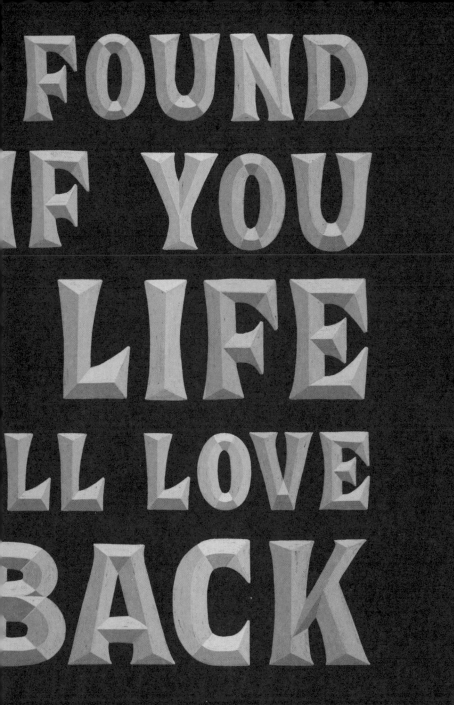

FOUND
IF YOU
LIFE
LL LOVE
BACK

Rubinstein

151

ABOUT THE AUTHOR

Elizabeth Gray is a lettering artist, illustrator, and muralist, but she's better known around the internet as @thegraytergood. She lives in Virginia with her husband and her cat, Emmy. Elizabeth enjoys creating content and client work from the comfort of her home studio. Her style of work is usually characterized by the use of a black + white color palette and is detailed, modern, and legible.

Elizabeth Gray

ACKNOWLEDGMENTS

To my husband of 7 years, Curtis: I wish that I was better at writing how I feel about you, or that this was as easy as the way you know my "I'm-putting-on-makeup voice," even over the phone. You're always the first to believe in me and to encourage me to make those big, beautiful, scary decisions, and you've truly held me up and helped me through the bear-of-a-process that is working on a book. Thank you for defending me, supporting me, and loving me without reserve. You'll always be my favorite homebody. <3

Mom and Dad: the older I get, the better sense of understanding I feel towards you both, and I love the way our relationship has grown and changed as I've grown up. But one thing that hasn't changed is the way you both encourage and support my decisions and dreams, and that means more to me than you can imagine. That kind of belief is why I've always felt the courage to pursue the things I felt passionate about and why I have the sort of creative career I've found myself in now. I'm sure it's easy to look at the experience of raising your kids through rose-colored glasses at this point, but I know that raising us was not easy at all. Thank you for everything. Hopefully seeing your names on the acknowledgments page in your daughter's book makes every late night and sacrifice seem a little more worth it.

ACKNOWLEDGMENTS

Brothers: thanks for helping raise me, keeping me tough, letting me dress one of y'all up in my Mickey Mouse pajamas and tutu (you know who you are), and for always making me feel protected and loved. People always told me that once I grew up, I'd appreciate my brothers more, and they were right. You're pretty cool after all. :p

To my best friends: you already know what I'm thinking, right? That's why we're best friends. I can't remember a time when you weren't there for me, and I'm so glad I don't have to live without you. Thank you for all the tears, laughter, coffee runs, frozen yogurt, and memories.

To the rest of my family, the in-laws, grandmas, and not-so-distant relatives: thank you for being there and for being a part of my family. From encouraging my many, many, many entrepreneurial exploits (soap-making, scarf-knitting, wedding cakery) to listening to me ramble on about clients and algorithms, you're a part of the reason why this book exists…even if you don't realize it.

To my editor, Lindsay, who I'm pretty convinced is the patron saint of patience when it comes to me and deadlines. You made this process fun and exciting and much

ACKNOWLEDGMENTS

less overwhelming than I thought it would be. Thank you for your calm presence, schedule-making, Dropbox organizing, and for just being your wonderful, fellow introvert/homebody self.

To Peter and Megan and the rest of the Blue Star team: thank you for encouraging me to go after this project, for being a part of this endeavor, for all the work that I know went into it that I haven't even seen, and for being so kind throughout this whole process. You're the first client to ask me about my mental health and that's when I knew I picked the right publisher.

Published by Blue Star Press

PO Box 8835, Bend, OR 97708

contact@bluestarpress.com | www.bluestarpress.com

Cover and Interior Artist: Elizabeth Gray
Developmental Editor: Lindsay Wilkes-Edrington
Designer: Megan Kesting

ISBN 9781950968381

Printed in China

10 9 8 7 6 5 4 3 2 1